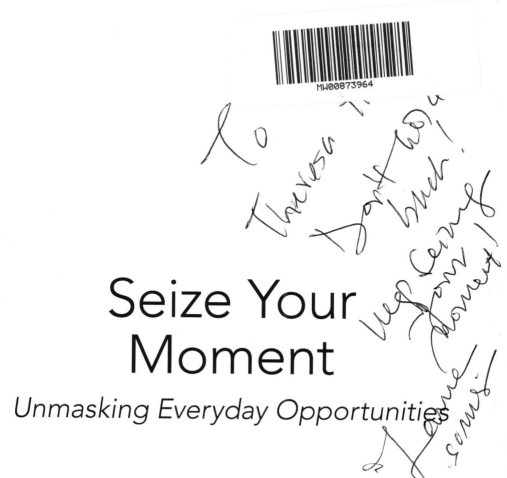

Seize Your Moment

Unmasking Everyday Opportunities

'LANRE SOMORIN MD

ISBN: 1978041527
ISBN-13: 9781978041523

I am delighted to dedicate this book to my lovely wife, Sade,
and to our two wonderful children, Tobi and Tami.
To Sade, thanks for the support, encouragement, and the sweetness you add to my
life. You are my best friend. Thanks for encouraging me to finish this book.
To Tobi, for being such a wonderful son. Your drive for excellence is truly inspiring.
It brings me a huge amount of joy to see what a fine young man you have become.
To Tami, my loving and affectionate daughter, who always looks out for her dad.

CONTENTS

INTRODUCTION

For I know the thoughts that I think toward you, says the Lord,
thoughts of peace, and not of evil, to give you a future and a hope.

—Jeremiah 29:11

God has a plan to bring us from where we are to where He has designed for us to be, but what often stands between us and God's plan is *opportunity*. We need to learn how to not only recognize but position ourselves to take advantage of God-given opportunities.

What is an opportunity? Dictionary.com (2017) defines an opportunity as

- an appropriate or favorable time or occasion
- a situation or condition favorable for attainment of a goal
- a good position, chance, or prospect, as for advancement or success

God's plan is to bring us to a place of promise, but this often involves us taking advantage of opportunities. Knowing God's promises and confessing them is not enough. We also need to know how to take advantage of the opportunities He brings our way. No matter what country we refer to, there are those who are prospering and those who are suffering.

Proverbs 12:27 (AMP) states that "the lazy man does not catch and roast his prey, but the precious possession of a wise man is diligence (because he recognizes opportunities and seizes them)." Consider James 2:14–17: "What does it profit, my brethren, if someone says he has faith but does not have works? Can faith save him? If a brother or sister is naked and destitute of daily food, and one of you says to them, 'Depart in peace, be warmed and be filled,' but you do not give them the things which are needed for the body, what does it profit? Thus also faith by itself, if it does not have works, is dead." We need to add corresponding actions to our faith, which often involves taking advantage of opportunity.

The goal of this book is to help you unmask the opportunities in your life. Opportunities surround us daily, but they are masked by the blinders we have on. This book will help you remove the roadblocks that have prevented you from taking advantage of the opportunities God has been bringing your way. A new day brings new opportunities, but you have to be positioned to take advantage of them.

In the book of Numbers 13, the children of Israel did not recognize the giants as an opportunity, so they ended up spending an extra forty years in the wilderness. Don't waste your time in the wilderness because you're running from giants. Step into God's will for your life.

I will discuss thirty-one keys that will help you unmask and take advantage of opportunities. By the time you've finished this book; my prayer is that you'll be able to step into the next season in your life by recognizing the opportunities you have where you are right now.

KEY 1

OPPORTUNITY COMES WHEN YOU PREPARE

Good fortune is what happens when opportunity meets with planning.

—*Thomas Edison*

William Arthur Ward has said that "men never plan to be failures; they simply fail to plan to be successful." Preparation is vital to being able to take advantage of opportunity. What are you going to do to prepare for the opportunities God will bring your way this year? You have prayed for a better year than last year, but what are you going to do to position yourself to recognize and take advantage of opportunities? George S. Clason stated that "opportunity is a haughty goddess who wastes no time with the un-prepared." Similarly, John Mason said that "few know when to rise to the occasion. Most only know when to sit down." God's plans for our lives are for good, and His blessings require obedience from us. In life, it is not just what you want that you get; you get what you prepare for. In Isaiah 1:19 we read, "If you are willing and obedient, you shall eat the good of the land."

If you are not prepared, you will not be able to recognize opportunity. Henry L. Hartman has said, "Success comes when preparation meets op-portunity," while the well-known TV personality Oprah Winfrey has said, "Doing the best at this moment puts you in the best place for the next moment." Mason also said that "great opportunity is where you are. Do not despise your own place and hour. The most important thing in our lives is what we are doing right now." Jonathan Swift said, "May you live all the days of your life," while Ralph Waldo Emerson said, "Write it on your heart that every day is the best day of your life."

The question is, what can you do to prepare for upcoming opportunities? You may not be able to take advantage of those opportunities now, but what are you doing to take advantage of them at a later date? What course do you need to take, what books do you need to read, which people do you need to meet, and where do you need to be geographically and mentally to take advantage of new opportunities? Some people say they don't have the time, or that it will take too long to position themselves correctly. But in five years' time, they may still be saying the same thing, wishing they had started the course or business five years earlier.

Stop having a short-term vision for your life, and think of the long-term impact of the decisions you make today. What can you do today to help position you for the future? Proverbs 16:1 says, "The preparations of the heart belong to man, but the answer of the tongue is from the Lord." God leaves the preparation to man. God will not prepare for you. Benjamin Franklin said that "by failing to prepare, you are preparing to fail." Whether your goal is to improve your health, your financial position, your academic standing, your career, or your relationship with your family, it is important to prepare. Preparation takes planning. It involves recognizing where you are and where you want to be and knowing what tools you need to get you there. Preparation involves knowing the order in which you must acquire the tools in order to get to where you need to be. Start preparing today, for tomorrow's opportunities.

KEY 2

So teach us to number our days that we may gain a heart of wisdom.

—Psalm 90:12

You need wisdom and understanding to take advantage of any opportunity. The opportunities God is bringing your way may not be available to you now because you have not acquired the necessary wisdom and understanding. It takes wisdom for you to know what you are meant to be doing and when you should be doing them. Wisdom helps you to number your days. You cannot move forward unless you have an understanding of where you are and where God wants you to be. Wisdom helps you to know what season you are in, and it helps you to discern the will of God for you.

James 1:1 instructs us to "count it all joy when you fall into various trials knowing that the testing of your faith produces patience…If any of you lack wisdom, let him ask of God." We need the wisdom of God to discern what a true opportunity is and whether that opportunity is consistent with God's plan for our lives. When we face trying times in our lives, God's Word says that we should seek wisdom. Very often, wisdom is the last thing people seek during trying situations. They just want to get out of the situation. They don't want to learn how they got themselves into the situation or what to do to prevent them from returning to it. If you're facing a problem in your job, for example, or if you're unemployed, you need wisdom to know how to seek the right job, the skills to thrive in the workplace, and the social skills necessary to get along with people. Having the favor of God on your life without people skills, will limit what God can do in your life.

First Corinthians 1:30 says, "But of Him you are in Christ Jesus, who became for us wisdom from God-and righteousness, and sanctification and redemption" The Bible says that Christ became for us wisdom from God. Proverbs 3:5–6 says, "Trust in the Lord with all your heart, and lean not on your own understanding; in all your ways acknowledge Him, and He shall direct your paths." We need understanding to be able to recognize and take advantage of opportunity.

You can change the neighborhood you live in (i.e., your zip code) simply by increasing your skill level. You may have been born into that neighborhood, but you don't have to remain there. In the Bible, Daniel and his friends had skills that separated them from their peers. Daniel 1:17 says, "As for these young men, God gave them knowledge and skill in all literature and wisdom: and Daniel had understanding in all visions and dreams." Daniel 1:20 says, "And in all matters of wisdom and understanding about which the king examined them, he found them ten times better than all magicians and astrologers who were in his entire realm." It is not enough to pray; you also need to have the right skill set. God was with Daniel and his friends, but they could not have been in that company without the necessary skill set. You need to invest in skill development and in understanding the trade.

The key to understanding is learning. Ecclesiastes 10:10 teaches us that "if the ax is dull, and one does not sharpen the edge, then he must use more strength; but wisdom brings success." This means that you need the right tools to get the job done—and if you must take the time to get the knowledge, information, skill, or edge you need in your field, then you should invest in it. If you want to get the right edge, then you need to sharpen the saw. The key to wisdom is knowing how to apply knowledge, which also includes taking advantage of opportunity. Understanding helps you to recognize opportunity, but it takes courage and wisdom to seize the opportunity.

KEY 3

OPPORTUNITY COMES IN THE MIDST OF ADVERSITY

My brethren, count it all joy when you fall into various trials,
knowing that the testing of your faith produces patience.

—James 1:2-3

Opportunity frequently comes in the midst of adversity. Very often in the Bible and in our lives, adversities present opportunities. Unfortunately, we tend to focus on the adversity instead of looking at the opportunity it presents. James 1:2 says, "My brethren, count it all joy when you fall into various trials, knowing that the testing of your faith produces patience." The Bible is telling us that, at the least, every trial presents an opportunity for our faith to be tested. This testing of our faith works patience, and this patience helps us to lack nothing.

In 1 Samuel 17:23–26, we see an example in the Bible where an adversity became an opportunity for a young boy in the story of David and Goliath. The adversity was that, when they saw Goliath, all the men of Israel fled from him and were dreadfully afraid. In verse 25 it said "It shall be that the man who kills him the king will enrich with great riches, will give him his daughter, and give his father exemption from taxes in Israel" In verse 26, "Then David spoke to the men who stood by him, saying, "What will be done for the man who kills this Philistine and takes away the reproach from Israel? For who is this uncircumcised Philistine, that he should defy the armies of the living God?" In verse 27, the people answered and said to him, "So shall it be done for the man who kills him." David asked what would be done for the person who killed Goliath. David saw it as an opportunity to find a spouse, to not pay taxes, and to be rich. That's why he asked what would happen to the person who killed Goliath. The Israelites saw Goliath as the end of life as they knew it; he saw it as an opportunity for his breakthrough.

What happens if, after praying, you realize that there is a Goliath to be killed? Will you proceed to kill Goliath or go back to prayer? David focused on what happened after Goliath, as opposed to focusing on the end of life as he knew it. The "Goliath" in your life could come in the form of a job that will place a demand on you, or it could be in the form of a problem that someone presents to you. David saw Goliath as an opportunity for his breakthrough.

Slay your Goliath!

Opportunity often comes as a problem for you or someone else. If you are focused on problems, then you will not recognize opportunity. David focused on what was on the other side of his Goliath rather than on seeing Goliath as the end of life. Could it be that the problem you're complaining about is an opportunity in disguise?

Your victory is on the other side of your fear. Very often when God gives you an instruction, fear shows up. If you allow fear to keep you from stepping out, then that fear will hinder you from your victory. You have to go through the fear—meaning that you have to do it afraid in order to get to where you need to be. What direction is God laying on your heart? What instruction, what opportunity, what idea? Don't allow fear to keep you from realizing God's promises.

God does not tell us all the things we'll face on our journey to our destiny. But He does expect us to be strong and bold. Most people give up because of the giants and opposition they meet on the way. But God wants us to press through the opposition so that we can reach our place of destiny.

Take courage! Consider Joshua 1:9: "Have I not commanded you? Be strong and of good courage: do not be afraid, nor be dismayed, for the Lord your God is with you wherever you go." It takes courage to take advantage of opportunity. You cannot kill a giant without a giant-killer mentality.

Joseph used his gift to solve a problem—interpreting the dreams of the butler and pharaoh—in Genesis 41:25–36. God put the solution to a nation's problem in the heart of His child. He can put the solution to the problem in your family, your company, your county, your state, and your nation inside you, His child. Bob Harris said, "Between you and anything significant will be giants in your path." If you want to get to the next level, you need to be willing to solve the problems of the next level, and that involves recognizing and taking advantage of opportunity. It may be something that scares you, something you don't have the money for, something you feel inadequate to do, or something that has a risk of failure, rejection, and humiliation. Opportunity does not come with a guarantee.

KEY 4

OPPORTUNITY COMES WHEN YOU WALK TOWARD YOUR PROMISE

..Why are we sitting here until we die?

—2 Kings 7:3

In 2 Kings 7: verses 3–4 say:

> "Now there were four leprous men at the entrance of the gate; and they said to one another, "Why are we sitting here until we die? If we say, 'We will enter the city': the famine is in the city, and we will die there. And if we sit here, we will die also. Now therefore, come let us surrender to the army of the Syrians. If they keep us alive, we shall live: if they kill us, we shall only die."

The four lepers were faced with the possibility of death, but they made a decision to walk toward the possibility of life. Could God be waiting on you to make a decision?

Behind these lepers was severe famine; in front of them was a hostile army. Staying in the same location was sure death because they were surrounded by famine. They asked themselves, "Why sit here until we die?" There were no easy decisions in this case, but they decided to walk toward the possibility of life rather than to stay in a place of inevitable death, and God used them to bring deliverance to His children.

Sometimes what we need to do is to walk toward our promise. Even when you have no certainty or guarantee of an outcome, you should walk toward your promise. For instance, the process of writing this book started in 2012. I started to write it little by little, but I never really set a time frame. I continued writing it through the years, taking breaks of three to six months at a time. In January 2017, the Lord encouraged me to finish the book. Later in the year, a member of my church walked up to me and said she felt impressed in her heart to ask, "What about the book?" She did not know I was writing a book. In October 2017, I had a discussion with my wife, and she emphasized how it was important for me to complete the book because there was a message in me that needed to get out to the world. I wasn't sure how I was going to get it published, but I decided to start making some phone calls. I called a marketer I knew, but she didn't get back to me. I contacted someone I'd met in the summer who'd written a book. He then sent me in the right direction. One thing led to the other, I paid the fee to the publisher, and at that point, I knew I was committed. I was walking toward my promise. I took one step at a time and here we are today.

We often want to figure things out five steps down the road, when God is saying to us that we should take the first step toward our promise. Five steps may be overwhelming, but the first step isn't as daunting. Take the first step toward your promise. Your direction is more important than your speed! Proverbs 3:5 teaches us to "trust in the Lord with all your heart, and lean not on your own understanding." Samuel Lover said, "Circumstances are the rulers of the weak, but they are the instruments of the wise." According to Mason, "If you like things easy, you will have difficulties, but if you like problems, you will succeed." Walk toward your promise, no matter the opposition.

KEY 5

OPPORTUNITY COMES WITH OBEDIENCE TO GOD'S INSTRUCTION

We have toiled all night and caught nothing;
nevertheless at your word...

—*Luke 5:5*

Peter was toiling all night yet he did not catch any fish. He had done all he knew to do, fishing wise. His expertise had told him when to fish, where to fish, and how to fish, and he was diligent in doing that. But Jesus came to him and told him a different way to fish, in a different place, and at a different time. Peter easily could have said, "Thanks for the concern, but I know there's no fish out there," instead he decided to be obedient to the Word. He decided that the Word was more powerful than his experience. You open the door to opportunity when you open your ears to God's instruction. His instruction is His provision. We have a responsibility to obey, not just hear.

Peter stated that "we have toiled all night...nevertheless at thy word I will let down the net for a catch." Even when it didn't make sense—it wasn't the right time for fishing, and they'd been there, done that, and were now washing their nets—he decided to obey the instruction of God.

How often does God tell us to do something, but we decide to do it our own way? God's blessings are connected to obedience to His instruction. The problem is that we want to figure out what the consequences are of the next move. We want to make sure that every move fits into our understanding. We want to decide when and how the breakthrough will come. But the "how" belongs to God. Our responsibility is to position ourselves to hear and to obey.

There are times when you will understand God's instruction and other times when you will not. Peter had toiled all night but then said, "Nevertheless, at thy word." His understanding told him that obeying Jesus' instruction would not work. The circumstances told him that doing so was not favorable. His experience, training, and trusted business partners all told him that what Jesus was saying was irrational. But he said, "Nevertheless, at thy word." That is how we ought to be as well. We need to say, "Nevertheless, at thy word." His obedience led to God's provision.

First Corinthians 2:9 states that "eye has not seen, nor ear heard, nor have entered into the heart of man the things which God has prepared for those that love Him. But God has revealed them to us by His Spirit." The Holy Spirit reveals to us God's instruction for our lives. God has prepared the way, but for you to experience it, you need to take advantage of opportunity. Very often we are competing for what other people have instead of what God has for us. The Holy Spirit has what it takes to help bring your future to pass. You need to walk in what is prepared. He reveals His plan for us through His spirit. Nobody can compete effectively for what God has in store for you. His revelation of His plan for you is reserved for that place of communion.

John 16:13-14 says, "However when He, the Spirit of truth has come, He will guide you into all truth: for He will not speak on His own authority, but whatever He hears He will speak; and He will tell you things to come "He will glorify Me, for He will take of what is Mine and declare it to you" The Holy Spirit is the key to fulfilling your purpose. He will unveil the truth of God's word to you. He also personalizes the word for you. He shows you how the word of God applies in your life. Proverbs 20:5 teaches us that "counsel in the heart of man is like deep waters, but a man of understanding will draw it out." Fellowshipping with God will help to draw out God's purpose for your life. You cannot fulfill your purpose apart from a relationship with God. The way he communicates that purpose is through his Spirit. Romans 8:14 says, "For as many as are led by the Spirit of God, these are the sons of God." We need to place priority on our time of fellowship, and we need to expect direction, counsel, instruction, and correction. We need to maintain a sensitive heart and meek spirit in order to receive instruction. Fellowship with the Holy Spirit comes in various forms. It can be in prayer, through worship, in meditation, or even in a worship service. The blessing is not in your ability to always understand God's instruction; it is in obedience to the instruction. The Bible states in First Samuel 15:22 that "..to obey is better than sacrifice"

KEY 6

OPPORTUNITY COMES WHEN YOU ARE CONNECTED TO A LOCATION

Now the Lord had said to Abram: "Get out of your country, from your family and from your father's house, to a land that I will show you."

—*Genesis 12:1*

Very often we find ourselves stuck in a rut because we have not obeyed the last instruction that God gave us. God told Abraham, "Get out of your country, from your family and from your father's house, to a land that I will show you. I will make you a great nation; I will bless you and make your name great. And you shall be a blessing." God told Abraham to leave the familiar: his family, his comfort zone, and his support system. He told him to go to a place that He would show him—somewhere unfamiliar but with a promise. As long as Abraham remained in Haran, he would not have prospered, because his blessing was connected to a different location. His father, Terah, had planned to go to the land of Canaan, but the Bible says in Genesis 11:31 that he decided to dwell in Haran instead. God knew that Abraham's blessing was not in Haran. He told him the promise, and that it was not where he was but in another location. Abraham had to move as instructed if he wished to experience the promise.

Are you prepared to stay in the familiar, with a guarantee of mediocrity, or to step into the unfamiliar, with a promise guaranteed by God? Very often we are comfortable where we are. We may have been in a particular profession or department for twenty years, but God is signaling that it's time for a change. You may have been in the same job for a lifetime, but God wants you to make a change. Your victory may be connected to a change in your location. You may have lived in a particular neighborhood for your whole life, but God is calling you to move. God wants to give you a revelation or opportunity that will change your life and environment. Sometimes it's important for you to move in order to change your perspective. In Genesis 15:1–5, God did not tell Abraham to look at the stars until he left Haran. You may be stuck because you haven't obeyed the last instruction God gave you. If God instructed you to move, the next instruction will come after you move. Otherwise, all you'll get is a reminder—move! You may not have seen yourself rising beyond a particular level academically, financially, or socioeconomically, but God then speaks to you and lets you know that it's time for a change. It is a change because it is different.

I told a colleague of mine once that, after moving an hour away from my old neighborhood, I was exploring the possibility of changing churches to somewhere closer. I told him that I hadn't found any I liked because they weren't like the other church I'd attended in the past. He said that that's why it's called a *change*. That's true. If it's the same, then it's not a change.

God spoke to Abraham again in Genesis 13:14 after he separated from Lot. Sometimes we need to separate ourselves from certain people and relationships to be able to hear clearly. What was the last thing God told you to do? Are you stuck in familiar territory because you can't deal with the uncertainty of God's direction?

Many people have the erroneous idea that God's direction always leads to a place of comfort immediately. Not necessarily. His direction may first lead us to a place of conflict, where we have to fight for the land. Very often, after we see the giants, we immediately want to look for another promised land. Don't walk past your promised land because you don't like the entrance!

What happens when God shows you a land, a position, a promotion, a business, or an idea that's beyond your current resources to attain? Do you retreat? Do you move along, seeking the next opportunity? Some people are wandering in the wilderness because they don't want to fight for the promised land. They are wandering in the wilderness because they're looking for a promised land without giants. They spend their lives waiting for a promised land that will fit into their preconceived image. Rather than asking God for the courage and boldness to take the promised land He has shown them, they instead seek another promised land. When you step out of the will of God, you begin to serve time. Consider Psalm 90:12, which says, "So teach us to number our days that we may gain a heart of wisdom."

The only way to avoid wandering in the wilderness is to follow God's plan for your life. The shortest distance between two points is a straight line. Obedience to God's will is the quickest way to your destiny. Detours from God's will simply make you serve time till you get back in His will. The good news is that you haven't been sentenced to forty years in the wilderness like the Israelites were. You can awaken and exit your wilderness just by applying the Word of God to your situation, and then acting on it.

Isaiah 60:1 says, "Arise, shine; for your light has come! And the glory of the Lord is risen upon you." As soon as light comes in, it is time to arise. Psalm 119:130 teaches us that "the entrance of Your words gives light; It gives understanding to the simple." As soon as the wisdom and understanding of God come into your heart, as soon as you receive God's direction, act on it, and you will take the first exit out of the wilderness and enter your place of promise. Hosea 4:6 says, "My people are destroyed for lack of knowledge." The more enlightened you are, the freer you become. Sometimes we face giants in our minds—human giants, giants of fear, financial giants, lack-of-resource giants. The blessing is connected to the location. Specifically, the blessing is connected to our obedience. While we do not determine the location of the blessing, we do determine the extent of our obedience.

KEY 7

OPPORTUNITY COMES AS HARD WORK

In all labor there is profit, but idle chatter leads only to poverty.

—Proverbs 14:23

Sometimes we look for opportunities that are easy. Goliath was not an easy opportunity. God blesses what you put your hands to. That is a statement I hear my pastor, Dean Brown, say often. Thomas Edison is thought to have said that "Opportunity is missed by most people because it is dressed in overalls and looks like work." Opportunity often involves working harder than you are now working. This may come as a surprise to many people who are looking for an easy win. They are waiting for their ship to come in. They may have given their offering or tithe to the church, so they expect a windfall with little to no effort. They feel that, if this is God, then they will not have to work harder because God knows they don't like to work too much.

After all, Jesus said, "My yoke is easy and my burden is light" (Matt. 11:30). But then second Thessalonians 3:10 teaches us that "for even when we were with you, we commanded you this: if anyone will not work, neither shall he eat." The Bible states that "money answers everything" (Eccles. 10:19). Opportunity may present itself as something that places a demand

KEY 8

OPPORTUNITY COMES IN THE FORM OF A RELATIONSHIP

He who walks with wise men will be wise,
but the companion of fools will be destroyed.

—Proverbs 13:20

You need to purposefully walk with wise men. Who inspires those who inspire you? We need to regularly evaluate the people we call friends. What is your benchmark? What company are you keeping? Small-minded people talk about other people. Who are you associating with? When was the last time they came up with an idea that improved your life? When was the last time they discussed an opportunity for your progress or said something to inspire you? The Bible says that a companion of fools shall be destroyed (Prov. 13:20).

That includes church folk. Who do you associate with at work, school, college, and even church? Are you running with people who are inspiring you, or are they keeping you stuck where you are? You do not surround yourself with wise men (and of course, wise women) by accident. You have to pursue wise men. Mediocrity and failure are what happen when you surround yourself with average people. Don't waste your time investing in relationships that are not heading anywhere. Relationships are investments of time. How well are your investments producing? We're going to have to give an account to God of our time, talents, and treasures.

How are you spending your time, and who are you spending it with? Proverbs 27:17 says, "As iron sharpens iron, so a man sharpens the countenance of his friend." How do you feel after spending time with your close friends? Do you feel sharpened, or do you feel dull? What specific skill sets do your close friends bring to your life? Would you want to be like your friend in five years? Choose your friends wisely. John Wooden said, "Five years from now, you are the same person except for the people you've met, and the books you've read." What influence do the people around you have?

When Satan wants to keep you static or make you backslide, he introduces you to a person. Are you positioned to identify that person? You should not have close friends by accident. They should be purposeful. Some friends may come into your life and may be a blessing initially, but then they begin to cause you to become stagnant. Some friends help maintain you in a particular stage of your life which may not be where you want to be stuck. You may have connected in grief, or you may have connected based on a common enemy or mutual interests. But God never speaks to two people the same way and at the same time, so you should never tie your destiny to someone else's, no matter how close you are.

Many people seek the opinions of the wrong people in order to make important decisions for their lives. Who are you asking for advice? What have they accomplished? Are they in the best position to advise you? Or are you too lazy to invest in relationships that will advance you? Powerful relationships will make you uncomfortable at first because they're designed to stretch you. You'll find out that when you are with people who know much more than you, you have to be quiet initially. If you find that you're the only one talking and giving advice in a relationship, then you've put a ceiling on your growth. If you're the star in your group of friends, then you need another set.

You need friends you can hang with and let your hair down with (so to speak). But you also need people who stretch you and make you uncomfortable in your field of endeavor or spiritual life. Those relationships have to be developed intentionally.

When God wants to move you to the next level, He also introduces you to a person. Are you positioned to identify that person? What relationship does God want you to start, rekindle, or invest more in? You need to look out for those relationships, and then nurture them. They may be in the form of a real person, or God can bring someone into your life through a book. You need to look out for the people God is bringing into your life and then invest in those relationships.

The most important relationship we can have is one with God, the creator. In John 3:16, the Bible says that "For God so loved the world that He gave His only begotten Son, that whosoever believes in Him should not perish but have everlasting life" The Bible asks in Mark 8:36 "What will it profit a man if he gains the whole world, and loses his own soul? God yearns for a relationship with humanity, and He sent His son, Jesus, to deliver us from our sins and to bring us into a relationship with Him. Without a relationship with our creator, we cannot achieve our full potential, because we are spirit, soul, and body, and all three parts must work correctly to reach our full potential.

If you would like to receive Christ into your life, a prayer at the end of this book will help you to do so; it will be the best decision you'll ever make.

KEY 9

OPPORTUNITY COMES WHEN YOU WORK AS A TEAM

For by wise counsel you will wage your own war,
and in a multitude of counselors there is safety.

—Proverbs 24:6

Proverbs 15:22 instructs us that "without counsel, plans go awry, but in the multitude of counselors they are established." How well do you work as a team? You need to be able to maximize the relationships in your life. Some people prefer to work alone, but certain unique opportunities can be achieved only when you work as a team. You need to develop the necessary skills to work as a team. Sometimes you are put in a team because of your work or school environment. Sometimes you may have to build a team based on your personal goals and visions. The proper use of experts is essential in helping you achieve your goals.

Being able to recognize the value of others and to create an atmosphere of bringing out the best in yourself and others is key to fulfilling your goals. If someone has a business opportunity, will he or she come to you? Do you have enough consistency, dependability, reliability, strength of character, and work ethic to be approached with a business idea? If your supervisor is looking for someone to promote, will you be on his or her list, or are you too busy gossiping about the supervisor? If your teacher is looking for someone to put in a leadership role, will you be one of the people the teacher considers, or are you the class clown?

Working as a team means being able to present ideas, recognize differences, and appreciate diversity, strengths, and unique talents. It means not always wanting to be the center of attention and allowing people to excel in their chosen fields. It involves overlooking people's shortcomings and keeping your eye on the bigger picture. It implies helping people to stay focused on a goal. Being a loner can significantly limit your God-given potential. God's grace can help you overcome any form of intimidation, fear, or shyness.

Opportunity comes when you work as a team.

KEY 10

OPPORTUNITY COMES AS A SIMPLE IDEA

The entrance of Your words gives light;
It gives understanding to the simple.

—Psalm 119:130

We need to see ourselves not only as consumers but also as problem solvers, creators, inventors, producers, investors, and owners. People have invented things that have become part of our normal, everyday lives. Sometimes opportunities come when we see ourselves as problem solvers, not just consumers. God, our Father, is the creator. The creative gene is inside us. Genesis 1:1 states: "In the beginning God created the heavens and the earth." Proverbs 8:12 says, "I, wisdom, dwell with prudence and find out knowledge of witty inventions." Everything we use today was once a thought or dream in someone's heart.

What stops you from coming up with the next product or improvement to a process? It doesn't have to be how to land a rocket on the moon—that's been done already. It may be how to improve on an existing product. Sara Blakely, the creator of Spanx, started her company in her twenties without advertising and with no debt. At one time she was the youngest self-made female billionaire on the *Forbes* list. She saw a need, and she met the need. Now, millions of people are thanking her for it.

Sometimes ideas come up because you want to improve your life. You then realize that it will improve many other people's lives as well. Many other people may have had the same idea but never considered it a priority. That's very important. It's not enough to have an idea; you need to focus on following through on that idea until it becomes a product. We need to see ourselves not only as consumers but also as problem solvers, creators, and inventors. This may involve solving a problem that is not in your job description. Even in your job, don't be limited by your job description. Be creative in your approach to problem solving. Think beyond the current constraints.

Opportunities come when you put yourself out there. Stop limiting yourself by your job description. Look for ways to be more valuable to your employer through your innovative thought process.

KEY 11

OPPORTUNITY COMES BY ANTICIPATING A NEED

*The ants are a people not strong, Yet they
prepare their food in the summer.*

—Proverbs 30:25

Opportunity comes when you anticipate a need. If you wait until the need is actually here, then you're most likely too late, because a solution has probably already been found. You need to be able to discern trends and seasons. This may be a need for a product, a device, or for knowledge in a particular field. It may be realizing that something is abundant in one place and in demand somewhere else. It could be a seasonal need; it could be a year-round need. You need to meet a need that other people are too busy to address but is of value to them.

What market are you studying? What field are you in? What need do you anticipate in the next year or over several years? In Genesis 41:32–36, Joseph, through his dream, anticipated a need, presented his own job description, and was hired for the job. When he interpreted the dream for Pharaoh, he anticipated the need for an administrator, and he expressed that need. God gave him a vision. Based on this, he identified the problem, created a solution, and came up with a job description for himself!

You will most likely be the person picked because you anticipated the need. Rather than complaining about your salary, anticipate a need and come up with a plan to meet that need. Sometimes opportunities come when you help people realize the need for a product or service that they may not otherwise be aware of. Leaders and CEOs are always looking for people who will anticipate a need and do something about it.

Even if you don't have the immediate answers, you have access to more than you are aware of. What area of progress are you focusing on, or are you just thinking of survival? What are you anticipating in your field, or are you just thinking of today? You may not know the answers, but you should be willing to find out. Zig Ziglar said, "You can have everything in life you want, if you will just help other people get what they want."

KEY 12

OPPORTUNITY COMES WHEN YOU REMOVE DISTRACTIONS

Where there is no revelation, the people cast off restraint.

—Proverbs 29:18

There are so many distractions today. TVs, smart phones, tablets, various media devices, and the internet are all designed to catch our attention all day. At times, we need to remove distractions—sometimes for a season and sometimes permanently. Some people are permanent distractions, and we need to remove them. You need to identify the people, places, and things that are preventing you from reaching your highest goals and full potential. When you remove distractions, you'll see opportunity where you are. Nature hates a vacuum. Things are filling your time right now because you don't know better.

As you increase learning, you'll recognize more opportunities, and your time will become more valuable. Your time cannot be more valuable to someone else than it is to you. Ecclesiastes 10:10 says, "If the ax is dull, and one does not sharpen the edge, then he must use more strength; but wisdom brings success." Sharpen the ax. When you invest in yourself, you'll increase your value, and people will pay you more for it. This often means removing distractions and making yourself more effective.

You need to constantly evaluate your effectiveness. This involves not only living in the moment but also taking time to look back and to learn from your experiences, reevaluating those who are close to you, paying attention to your work habits, and making the necessary changes so that you will become more effective in reaching your goal.

Removing distractions presupposes that you have a goal to meet. If you don't have a goal, then you really can't be distracted. Distraction comes to move you away from your goal or calling. You need to have a clear view of where you're heading in order to remove distractions, and you must stick to that clear view. What you see will depend in large part on what you're looking for. To one person, the world looks desolate, dull, and empty; to another, the same looks rich, interesting, and full of meaning. Mason said, "Position yourself to receive, not resist."

How you see things outside depends on how you see things inside. Proverbs 23:7 says, "For as he thinks in his heart, so is he." When you're positioned in the right way, opportunity presents itself. Expect something good to happen. That expectation will energize your dreams.

Proverbs 29:18 (KJV) teaches us that "where there is no vision, the people perish: but he that keepeth the law, happy is he." Do you see what God is doing in your life? Consider Jeremiah 29:11(KJV): "For I know the thoughts that I think toward you, saith the Lord, thoughts of peace, and not of evil, to give you an expected end." You have an expected end. It is never too late to start thinking creatively.

For example, a colleague of mine who is seventy-eight years old just began to incorporate the field of tele psychiatry into his practice. He did not believe he was too old to start thinking creatively. He converted an old bedroom in his home into a tele psychiatry office and had the equipment set up there. He is able to sit in the comfort of his home, see patients in other locations, and get paid the same as if he was physically there. If we are to function at our potential, we need to use our imagination. We've got to have a dream in the first place if we're going to make a dream come true.

You're never too poor until you're too poor to dream.

KEY 13

OPPORTUNITY COMES WHEN YOU ASK THE RIGHT QUESTIONS

But when he came to himself, he said, "How many of my father's hired servants have bread enough and to spare, and I perish with hunger!"

—*Luke 15:17*

The prodigal son had squandered his inheritance in riotous living and was now living in a pigpen, sharing the food allocated to the pigs. He decided to reason through the process. He asked himself how many of his father's hired servants had food to eat as well as to spare. The Bible says he came to himself. Nobody can "come to yourself" for you. You have to come to yourself by asking the right questions. Why are you doing what you are doing? Are you living at your full potential, or are you surrounded by "pigs"? Meaning, are you surrounded by people who are making you live way below your potential? Does your life reflect your heavenly father? Is there room for improvement? (There always is.)

As Bishop Oyedepo noted in his book *The Force of Freedom* (1996), "Sometimes you don't pray for a breakthrough, you think through a breakthrough." That's what the prodigal son did—he thought through a breakthrough. He asked himself the right questions. He asked himself what he was doing among pigs while his father's servants had more than enough to eat. He realized he was living way below his potential. He realized there was a relationship (the one with his father) that once restored, could change his standard of living immediately. He retraced his steps and decided he could do something about the rut he was in. He just looked at the consequences of his actions and identified one thing he could do to change his circumstances. He did not blame anyone, including his friends with whom he'd blown his inheritance. He did not allow pride to get in the way of his breakthrough. He said, "I will arise," and he did.

What questions are you asking yourself? Have you evaluated your life, your decisions (and their consequences), your surroundings, and what will happen if you don't do anything differently? What conclusions have you come to, or are you too busy to reflect on your life? Are you too busy blaming family, friends, the economy, the president, or political parties? Like the prodigal son, we need to evaluate our lives by asking the right questions. Once we come up with a decision, we need to act on it. Acting on a decision changed the prodigal son's situation instantaneously. Sometimes God will drop the seed of change into your life in the form of a question. You need to follow that question through to your breakthrough. What question has God planted in your heart?

You need to think differently. You must assess your life on a regular basis. This applies to your marriage, finances, relationships, purpose, love walk, faith walk, prayer life, your involvement in church, job, school—everything. You must anticipate what is at the end of the road you're on and read the signs along the way. Why are you on the wrong road but expecting to get to the right destination? As Matthew 7:13–14 notes, "Enter by the narrow gate; and broad is the way that leads to destruction, and there are many who go in by it. Because narrow is the gate and difficult is the way which leads to life, and there are few who find it." God does not change your destination; He places you on the right road. The wrong road will never lead to the right destination, no matter how fast you go on it.

Some people need patience to stay on the right road. Other people need to get off the wrong road and get on the right road. If you're in the wrong relationship, then get away from it. If your marriage is heading in the wrong direction, then seek help. Don't ask God to help change the outcome of bad decisions you are about to make. We need to take inventory of our lives, our relationships, and our finances.

If you depend on others to ask questions about you before you make the necessary changes, you are officially in trouble. That's what parole officers and judges are for! You need to learn to read road signs. Most people will watch you self-destruct and not tell you that you're on the wrong road. Philippians 3:14 says, "I press toward the goal for the prize of the upward call of God in Christ Jesus." Paul knew what prize he was reaching for. What is the prize of your high calling? You cannot stumble on a prize you are not reaching for.

You can tell where people are going to be in five years by the questions they are asking themselves now:

- Where do I want to be five years from now?
- Where do I want my marriage to be five years from now?
- Why do I want to be financially free?
- Why do I want to financially support my church?
- If I were asked to manage someone with my identical skills, what would I say to him or her?
- Do I have written goals for the year?

What kind of questions are you asking yourself?

KEY 14

OPPORTUNITY COMES BY TAKING STOCK OF YOUR GIFT

A man's gift makes room for him and brings him before great men.

—Proverbs 18:16

We need to take stock of the gift that we have. Consider Philemon verse 6: "That the sharing of your faith may become effective by the acknowledgment of every good thing which is in you in Christ Jesus." Stop talking about your weaknesses and what you cannot do. Your faith becomes effectual by acknowledging every good thing that is in you in Christ Jesus. How much time do you spend acknowledging good things, and how much time do you spend disqualifying yourself and acknowledging your weaknesses? Start focusing on what you can do and what God has placed in you.

Heaven has no recalls, so you came fully equipped and functioning. Proverbs 18:16 says, "A man's gift makes room for him, and brings him before great men." If you are not hanging around great men (or women), it's because you haven't tapped into your gifts. The Bible says your gift will make room for you. What does that mean? It means your gift will create opportunities for you that otherwise would not have been provided. It means it elevates you, distinguishes you, makes you exceptional, and causes a demand to be made available for your product. It means you come out of obscurity—you come out of the crowd, the background noise, the queue, or the order. It means you stop living in a life of constraints and go instead to a place of roominess. Genesis 26:22 says that "And he moved from there and dug another well, and they did not quarrel over it. So he called it's name Rehoboth, because he said "for now the Lord has made room for us, and we shall be fruitful in the land." This means that your gift will bring you on stage. In Exodus 4:2, God said to Moses, "What is that in your hand?" He is saying the same to you.

The only place you can start is from where you are and with what you have. In *Conquering an Enemy Called Average*, Mason mentioned that many people focus on what they cannot do instead of on what they can do. Mike Murdock noted that God has placed in you everything you need to be the person He has designed you to be. You must have faith in what God has placed in you. God will often multiply what you have in your hand, but you need to know *what* you have in your hand.

Stop overvaluing others and undervaluing yourself. We often talk about how big God is, but we act like He left something out when He created us. God did not leave anything out; He left everything you need on the inside of you in seed form. The Bible says we are complete in Him. Colossians 2:10 says, "And you are complete in him, who is the head of all principality and power." God will supply anything you need. First Corinthians 2:16 says, "For who has known the mind of the Lord that He may instruct him? But we have the mind of Christ." First John 4:4 tells us that "greater is he that is in you, than he that is in the world."

You have access to the wisdom of God and can overcome anything in this life, according to First Corinthians 1:30. What you need to do is to stir up that gift. Consider Second Timothy 1:6–7: "Therefore I remind you to stir up the gift of God which is in you through the laying on of my hands. For God has not given us a spirit of fear, but of power and of love and of a sound mind." The things that cloud the gift have to do with an unsound mind and strife. Make sure you keep strife out of your life. We will discuss this more in a later chapter.

Take an inventory of your gifts. What do you do well? What gift do you need to develop? What environment do you need to develop that gift? How can you exercise your gift? Who are the mentors in your life who can help guide your gift? God will not do for you what He has equipped you to do. God has put the right equipment in you. You need to reign in this life with it.

Your gift will bring you out of obscurity.

KEY 15

OPPORTUNITY COMES BY BELIEVING YOU HAVE A BETTER TOMORROW

But the path of the just is like the shining sun,
that shines ever brighter unto the perfect day.

—Proverbs 4:18

You have to believe in a better tomorrow to take advantage of opportunity. Many people fail to take advantage of opportunity because they don't believe they have a better tomorrow. They don't have a vision of a better tomorrow. Expectation is a requirement for taking advantage of opportunity. As Proverbs 29:18 (KJV) says, "Where there is no vision, the people perish." Without a vision of a better tomorrow, you cannot effectively take advantage of opportunities. Living life without a vision is like serving time. Hope is a confident and joyful expectation.

Proverbs 24:14 (KJV) says, "So shall the knowledge of wisdom be unto thy soul: when thou hast found it, then there shall be a reward, and thy expectation shall not be cut off." The expectation of the righteous shall not be cut off. Consider Jeremiah 29:11: "For I know the thoughts that I think toward you, says the Lord, thoughts of peace and not of evil to give you a future and a hope." God's plan is to bring us to a place of hope in our final outcome. Proverbs 4:18 says, "But the path of the just is like the shining sun, that shines ever brighter unto the perfect day." If you're not at that perfect day, your light is still shining and will get brighter.

Hebrews 11:1 teaches us that "faith is the substance of things hoped for." Some people have lost hope for a better tomorrow due to past losses, repeated disappointments, failed relationships, and unmet expectations. Don't let the disappointments of the past cause you to lose hope for tomorrow. Lamentations 3:21–23 says, "This I recall to my mind, therefore I have hope. Through the Lord's mercies we are not consumed, because His compassions fail not. They are new every morning; great is Your faithfulness." This means that His faithfulness is strong enough to give you a new beginning every day. Your past disappointments are not strong enough to be permanent unless you allow them to be. We need to envision a brighter tomorrow.

If your vision does not scare you, then you are officially in a rut.

If your vision does not excite you, then you have reached stagnation.

If your vision does not irritate some people, then you are likely compromising.

It is time to hope again. You need hope in order to be able to walk in faith. Hebrews 11:1 says, "Now faith is the substance of things hoped for, the evidence of things not seen." We've got to have a dream if we're going to make a dream come true.

KEY 16

OPPORTUNITY COMES WHEN YOU HAVE A GRATEFUL HEART

Enter into His gates with thanksgiving
and into His courts with praise.

—*Psalm 100:4*

Gratitude is key in recognizing and maintaining fellowship with God, which in turn opens the door to opportunities in your life. Psalm 103:1–5 reads, "Bless the Lord O my soul; and all that is within me, bless his Holy name! Bless the Lord O my soul, and forget not all His benefits. Who forgives all your iniquities, Who heals all your diseases, Who redeems your life from destruction, Who crowns you with loving kindness and tender mercies, Who satisfies your mouth with good things, So that your youth is renewed like the eagle's." Very often, we are so focused on our problems that we forget the blessings of God in our lives. We need to remember His blessings and benefits in order to position ourselves to experience more of them.

We also need to take time to truly recall these benefits and appreciate them. If you cannot recall, then you cannot walk in hope. Lamentations 3:21:

"This I recall to my mind and therefore I have hope." You need a good recall to be thankful. Some people have selective recall—they only recall problems. But the Bible encourages us to recall God's blessings, because this is what gives us hope. You have a choice as to what you choose to recall. If you can't recall, you'll have a "What have you done for me lately?" attitude. If you do not appreciate God's blessings today, how will you have hope for a better future? Ward has said that "the more we count the blessings we have, the less we crave the luxuries we haven't."

Psalm 100:4–5 reads: "Enter into His gates with thanksgiving and into His courts with praise. Be thankful to Him and bless His name. For the Lord is good: His mercy is everlasting and His truth endures to all generations." We are encouraged to enter into His gates with thanksgiving and into His courts with praise. If we are to fellowship with God, then we need to enter into His presence, and the way we do that is through thanksgiving and praise, not by murmuring and complaining. Some people don't experience the true fellowship of God because all they do when they commune with God is murmur, complain, and talk about all that is going wrong in their lives. Ward said that "a complaining tongue reveals an ungrateful heart." Thanksgiving opens your heart to receive from God. When you thank God for what He has done, you will see more reasons to thank Him. Thanksgiving keeps you in fellowship with God. It also helps to prevent you from being bogged down with the problems in life, because it prevents you from having tunnel vision and allows you to see God's goodness in the midst of problems.

The psalmist mentioned in Psalm 27:13 that "I would have lost heart, unless I had believed to see the goodness of the Lord in the land of the living." Thanksgiving helps you to see God's goodness no matter how dark the situation is, because doing so brings God on the scene. It also helps you to remember what He has done for you. When you remember where He brought you from, it strengthens your faith to know He can bring you through what you're going through. Thanksgiving gives you staying power when you're standing in faith. Isaiah 40:31 states, "But those who wait on the Lord shall renew their strength: they shall mount up with wings as eagles, they shall run and not be weary, they shall walk and not faint."

Psalm 22:3 (KJV) reads: "But thou art holy, O thou that inhabits the praises of Israel." While you have an attitude of thanksgiving, you remain in fellowship with God. While you remain in fellowship with God through thanksgiving, you are open to his blessings and opportunities.

KEY 17

OPPORTUNITY COMES WHEN YOU ACT PURPOSEFULLY TO BE A BLESSING

It is more blessed to give than to receive.

—Acts 20:35

As Isaiah 55:10 teaches us, that rain from heaven will "give seed to the sower and bread to the eater". We always need to look for opportunity to sow seed so we can create opportunities to reap a harvest. Acts 20:35 says, "It is more blessed to give, than to receive." More blessings come to you when you give than when you receive. If we truly believed this, we will look for opportunities to be a blessing to others. God blesses you so that you can be a blessing in turn. As Luke 6:38 tells us, "Give, and it shall be given to you: good measure, pressed down, shaken together, and running over will be put into your bosom." This means that what you give never comes back to you the same way. It comes back in a way that is pressed down, shaken together, and running over. No wonder it is more blessed to give than to receive. In Genesis 12:2, God told Abraham, "I will make you a great nation: I will bless you and make your name great: And you shall be a blessing." God's purpose in blessing Abraham and making his name great was to make him a blessing. Many want to be blessed and have great names, but they do not want to be a blessing themselves.

If you act purposefully to be a channel, God will bring his blessings through you. Everybody has something to give. Some people think that because they are not wealthy, they have nothing to give. Acting purposefully to be a blessing has nothing to do with how much money you have; it has to do with whether you have the heart of a giver. The Bible states that God loves a cheerful giver. You can give of your time, your talent, or your treasure. You can speak a comforting word, make a call to someone you haven't seen in a while, or pay for groceries for someone in the store who's struggling to pay. You have abundant opportunities to be a blessing to the people around you. The issue is whether or not you're looking for those opportunities. Many people want to be on the receiving end of blessings instead of being on the giving end. Opportunities will come your way when you act purposefully to be a blessing.

You need to act purposefully to be a blessing—not only to your family but also to your friends, your church, and your community. We need to recognize that the gift that God has given us is not only for us but also for others. Consider Ephesians 2:10: "For we are His workmanship, created in Christ Jesus for good works, which God prepared beforehand that we should walk in them." You are created to walk in good works. Isaiah 61:1 says, "The Spirit of the Lord God is upon me, because the Lord has anointed me." You need to also identify the people whom you are called to reach.

Second Corinthians 5:14 says, "For the love of Christ constrains us." Whom do you feel constrained to reach out to? You are not called to reach out to everyone. Then pray for the anointing of God to flow through you to reach that person. Don't say that you're waiting on the Lord to know whom to reach; be a blessing to those around you first while you wait for more specific direction. Start each day by asking God to open your eyes to opportunities to be a blessing that day.

KEY 18

OPPORTUNITY COMES WHEN YOU SEE FAILURE AS DELAY, NOT AS DEFEAT

Failure should be our teacher, not our undertaker.

—William Arthur Ward

Failure is delay, not defeat. Some of us are stuck where our last failure happened, and we have camped out there. Failure is an event, not a person. If you're going to be able to position yourself to prosper, you have to be willing to take responsibility for failure. As Denis Waitley has said, "It is a temporary detour, not a dead end." The fear of failure is a major reason that people don't recognize opportunity. Consider Philippians 3:13–14: "Forgetting those things which are behind and reaching forward to those things which are ahead, I press toward the goal for the prize of the upward call of God in Christ Jesus."

You need to develop the habit of forgetting those things that are behind you so you can press forward. You cannot spend your life asking, "Why did it happen to me?" At some point, it's time to move on. God has a plan that is better than your pain. God has not stopped releasing His daily blessings. Psalm 68:19 says, "Blessed be the Lord, who daily loads us with benefits, The God of our salvation!" Recognize the truth that failure is an event, and avoid thinking that it is a person. Failure is simply something that happened and should never be tied to the reputation of an individual. Don't tie your identity to failure.

The Joyce brothers have said that "the only people who don't make mistakes are the people who don't make anything." The responsibility for success comes with the possibility of failure. Every endeavor carries risk. We cannot live a productive life if we're afraid to take risks. Today is a new day, and you should never encumber its opportunities with the dread of the past. You should always be in a position to receive a blessing. You should not waste a moment on the regrets of yesterday.

Lamentations 3:22 says, "Through the Lord's mercies we are not consumed, because His compassions fail not. They are new every morning: Great is Your faithfulness." Holding onto the past prevents us from receiving today. God's mercies and compassions are strong enough to give you a new beginning each day. You need to let go and let God. All successful people have experienced failure in one way or another, but they didn't let it stop them from trying again.

KEY 19

OPPORTUNITY COMES WHEN A DEMAND IS PLACED ON YOU

Go in this might of yours, and you shall save
Israel from the hand of the Midianites.

—Judges 6:14

This demand can come from others (i.e., active), or you can place it on yourself (passive). At times, you may be suddenly thrust into a leadership position because of an emergency or crisis, and you rise to the occasion. We see this in the life of Gideon in Judges 6:12: "The Angel of the Lord appeared to him, and said to him, "The Lord is with you, you mighty man of valor!" Judges 6:14 goes on: "Then the Lord turned to him and said 'Go in this might of yours, and you shall save Israel from the hand of the Midianites. Have I not sent you?"

God called him to lead in a time of crisis. He did not feel qualified to save the Israelites from the hand of their enemies, the Midianites. Verse 15 says, "So he said to Him, 'O my Lord, how can I save Israel? Indeed my clan is the weakest in Manasseh, and I am the least in my father's house." He eventually responded to the demand that was placed on him, and he rose to the occasion. Verse 27 says, "So Gideon took ten men from among the servants and did as the Lord said to him."

There are times, however, when you need to put that demand on yourself. God's perfect will is not going to be accomplished simply by waiting for people to put a demand on you. At times, you need to initiate something. Don't take the easy road. Set a goal and set a deadline. Gail Vaz-Oxlade has said that "a goal without a deadline is just a dream." You need to set a goal that places a demand on you: something that causes you to bring together all your creative processes; something that forces you to look deep within and to bring out the best in yourself and other people.

Several years ago, I put a demand on myself to be recognized as an expert in the field of addiction in Orange County, New York. I decided to conduct a symposium, so I brought several speakers together, in addition to myself, to address the problem of the opioid abuse and synthetic marijuana crisis in the community. It was a huge success. Several years later, people see me in the community and say they came to one of my training sessions. I remember that it was after I planned to have the seminar that I began to have creative ideas about the content, and God began to lead me to the right people to speak at the conference. I went to a conference in New York City on the topic, and I was really inspired by one of the speakers, who was a toxicologist. I felt he would be perfect to speak at the conference. I approached him after the conference and mentioned that I wanted him to be a speaker at a symposium I was holding. He apologized, saying that he wouldn't be able to come because he'd be out of the country at the time, but he asked his colleague if he would speak. His colleague accepted, did a phenomenal job, and did not charge anything! If I had not stepped out in faith, I would not have had access to these people.

Don't wait for others to place a demand on your growth. Place it on yourself. Initiate something. In 2008, I decided to place a demand on myself by opening a private substance abuse outpatient rehabilitation facility in Monroe, New York. It was a daunting task at the time because it was self-funded. I took it step by step. I downloaded the application form and began to complete it. I needed to submit over twenty policies, hire all the required staff, train the staff in the policies, secure a location, furnish it, and pass an initial inspection before I would get the operating license and see my first patient. And I had a full-time job at the time. I fulfilled the requirements and opened the substance abuse clinic in November 2010. I grew through the process. Nobody asked me to do it; it was a goal of mine to see a substance abuse rehab that offered faith-based approaches, evidence-based counseling, and medication-assisted treatment. In 2010, the Exodus Clinic opened and operated till 2016 with excellence.

Don't just settle for where you are. Opportunities can be created. Don't just wait for your ship to come in. Build your own ship.

Mason made the following statements in *Conquering an Enemy Called Average*:

- "You cannot become what you are destined to be by remaining where you are."
- "When patterns and traditions are broken, new opportunities come together."
- "Defending your faults and errors only shows you have no intention of quitting."
- "All progress is due to those who are not satisfied to leave well enough alone."

When you are approached with an opportunity for advancement, don't let it pass by. Rise to the occasion. When you see an opportunity to exercise leadership, step up. Opportunity comes in response to a demand.

KEY 20

OPPORTUNITY COMES WHEN YOU DO IT AFRAID

God has not given us a spirit of fear.

—Second Timothy 1:7

Where there is opportunity, there is often danger. You cannot wait for the fear to pass before you step out. At times, you will need to step out even when you are fearful. Some people wait for the fear to leave before they do things. But it is in doing things despite the fear that causes the fear to leave. Fear is the result of listening to the giants. Faith is the result of listening to God. Consider Second Timothy 1:7: "For God has not given us a spirit of fear, but of power and of love and of a sound mind."

Never allow fear to determine the boundaries of your life. The just shall live by faith (Second Corinthians 5:7). The Bible details an account of Peter walking on water in Matthew 14:28-31, "And Peter answered Him and said "Lord if it is you, command me to come to You on the water." So He said "Come." And when Peter had come down out of the boat, he walked on the water to go to Jesus. But when he saw the wind was boisterous, he was afraid and beginning to sink he cried out saying 'Lord Save me" And immediately Jesus stretched out His hand and caught him, and said to him: O you of little faith, why did you doubt?" When Peter stepped out of the boat, he did it afraid, but he still walked on water—until he shifted his focus to the winds, and then he began to sink. We need to keep our focus on the God who gave the promise. The enemy uses fear to keep us from our destiny. The fact that fear shows up does not mean we have to stop. Fear is a weapon of the enemy. The Bible says in Isaiah 54:17: "No weapon formed against you shall prosper." The way fear prospers is by keeping you from doing what you are afraid of doing. Do it afraid and the fear will leave.

I remember when I was presented with an opportunity to do some extra work. I was fearful because I had not worked that shift before and was worried about my ability to come up to speed in a very short time and to make important decisions about patients. After my first day on the four-day assignment, the fear had dissipated because I'd shown up and taken on the challenge. I realized it was not as bad as I'd thought. God spoke to my heart on the last day, saying, "Your victory is on the other side of your fear"—meaning I had to push through the fear. The fact that you fear does not mean that God is not involved.

Very often when God asks us to do things that are outside our comfort zone, or that we feel unqualified or inadequate to do, our natural response is to be fearful. That is not where the story ends, however. You have a decision to make. Will you allow fear to keep you from making a decision to obey God, or will you do it afraid, in obedience to God? Many people are waiting for the fear to leave so that they will feel peace and can then obey God. But it does not have to be that way. There are times when you need to do it afraid! There are times when you need to step out, even when there are giants. That's what the children of Israel faced. They saw giants and decided that that Canaan was not the right promised land. They thought that the fact that they had to fight for something meant it was not God leading them. But the opposite is true. When God has promised you something, you still have to go out and possess it. Sometimes that means dispossessing something else. In order to possess what we need, we need to dispossess fear, insecurity, low self-esteem, confusion, double-mindedness, and contrary voices. Our warfare is not against flesh and blood (unless you are in the army) but against principalities and powers (First Corinthians 10:4).

We may not be fighting physical giants, but spiritual giants. Second Corinthians 10:4–5 says, "For the weapons of our warfare are not carnal but mighty in God for pulling down strongholds, casting down arguments and every high thing that exalts itself against the knowledge of God, bringing every thought into captivity to the obedience of Christ." We are going against mental strongholds of fear and insecurity, casting down arguments of failure and defeat, and bringing every contrary thought to the obedience of Christ. The warfare we face is in the mind; it is not physical. When there is a promise to possess something and fear shows up, the way we deal with that fear is by engaging spiritual forces to dethrone these strongholds in our minds. We do not wait for a feeling. Second Corinthians 5:7 notes, "For we walk by faith, not by sight." We step out on the promise of God, even if fear is present.

KEY 21

OPPORTUNITY COMES WHEN YOU WALK IN FORGIVENESS

Forgive us our sins for we also forgive everyone who is indebted to us.

—Luke 11:4

Opportunity comes when you walk in forgiveness. Forgiveness is a choice. We have many reasons for getting offended during the course of our days and lives. It takes two things to get offended, however: it takes someone to offend you, and it takes you to be offended. Unforgiveness puts you in bondage, while the one who committed the offense may be walking free. The person who offended you may not even be aware that he or she did so.

Matthew 18:23–35 discusses a parable of a servant who owed his master ten thousand talents (the currency of the time), and he did not have anything to pay. His lord commanded him to be sold, along with his wife and children and all that he had, and for payment to be made. The servant begged and asked for mercy. His lord was moved with compassion, and he freed him and forgave him his debt. The Bible states that the same servant went out and found one of his fellow servants who owed him a fraction of what his master had forgiven him (a hundred pence); he laid his hands on him, took him by the throat, and said, "Pay me what you owe!" The other servant pleaded, but he would not have mercy on him and cast him into prison till he paid his debt. The other servants saw what the man had done and told the master. The Bible says that his lord was angry and delivered the servant to the tormentors until he paid all that was due to him. It then concludes in verse 35: "So My heavenly Father also will do to you if each of you, from the heart, does not forgive his brother his trespasses."

James 3:16 (KJV) states, "For where envying and strife is, there is confusion and every evil work." This happens all too often in marriages, where people allow strife into their home because they feel they have been wronged and deserve to walk in unforgiveness. Strife is spiritual; it opens the door to the enemy to cause confusion and "every evil work." Is it really worth walking around in confusion and being a sitting target of the enemy because someone offended you? Once strife comes in, love goes out, and the Bible says that faith works through love (Gal. 5:6). The Bible also states that our prayers are hindered as a couple when we do not dwell as heirs together of the grace of life (1 Peter 3:7). Don't allow the enemy into your affairs due to strife and unforgiveness.

There are times when you need to forgive people—not because they deserve it, but because you deserve it. You deserve to walk free from confusion.

You deserve to walk free from every evil work.

You deserve to have your prayers answered.

You deserve to live in a peaceful home.

Forgiveness opens the door to God's blessings; unforgiveness opens the door to every evil work. The Lord's Prayer in Luke 11:4 says, "And forgive us our sins, for we also forgive everyone who is indebted to us, and lead us not into temptation, but deliver us from the evil one." If we are not willing to forgive, we will not be forgiven. You need to be forgiven more than you want to hold on to unforgiveness. Some people suffer from mental anguish as a result of unforgiveness.

Forgiveness has nothing to do with whether the offender deserves it or the extent of the offense; it has to do with whether you're willing to give up your freedom to remain in bondage. Forgiveness has to do with how much confusion and evil work you're willing to put up with. It has to do with how much of an unanswered prayer life you're willing to put up with.

Ephesians 4:31 says, "Let all bitterness, wrath, and anger, and clamor, and evil speaking, be put away from you with all malice: and be ye kind to one another, tenderhearted, forgiving one another, even as God in Christ forgave you." If God is willing to forgive, then what's your excuse? We have no acceptable excuse for unforgiveness with God. Opportunity comes when we walk in forgiveness because a lot of opportunities come through relationships.

Opportunities also come as we step out in faith. (Galatians 5:6 discusses faith working through love.) Now, if faith works by love, then we cannot successfully take advantage of opportunities if we are in unforgiveness. Unforgiveness stops everything and makes time stand still, because you will not be making progress. It's like a cancer that can eat you up from the inside. Mark 11:25 says, "And when ye stand praying, forgive, if you have anything against anyone, forgive him, that your Father in heaven may also forgive you your trespasses." Paul Boese has said, "Forgiveness does not change the past, but it does enlarge the future." Forgiveness gives you the opportunity to walk in God's blessings, unhindered by the burden of offense.

KEY 22

OPPORTUNITY COMES WHEN YOU CONSIDER YOUR HIGH CALLING

I press toward the goal for the prize of the upward call of God in Christ Jesus.

—Philippians 3:14

Stop comparing yourself with others, and start comparing your progress with your high calling. What has God placed in you? Consider Philippians 3:13–14: "Brethren, I do not count myself to have apprehended; but one thing I do, forgetting those things which are behind and reaching forward to those things which are ahead, I press toward the goal for the prize of the upward call of God in Christ Jesus." You have an upward call of God upon your life. Don't let your environment and peers define you. Let God's expectations define you.

Your goal should be for Him to say, "Well done, thou good and faithful servant." You need to assess where you are in relation to your high calling. Where does God expect you to be in relation to His purpose for your life? The Bible commands us to press toward the mark of the high calling of God in Christ Jesus. The mark of the high calling should be strong enough to pull you toward it. For that to happen, you need to focus on it and keep it in view. This prevents you from getting stuck in a rut. Do not focus on the past or allow the regrets of yesterday to keep you stuck. There is a reason you were apprehended in Christ Jesus. You should not feel you have arrived or as if there is not much more to life.

You should always be pressing toward your high calling in Christ. You would not be alive if God did not have something more in store for you. God has a higher calling for you in Christ Jesus. You need to see and appreciate that higher calling. Doing so also helps you not to compare yourself to others. You don't have the same high calling as anyone else. It is unique to you. Your calling is not necessarily the same as your occupation. You should never lose sight of your high calling, and it should permeate everything you do in your personal life, relationships, and occupation.

You don't have the same set of gifts as anyone else. You don't have the same race to run as anyone else. You need to focus on your own goal and run your own race. Your goal should not be to outdo others but to outdo yourself and go further in your calling.

KEY 23

OPPORTUNITY COMES WHEN YOU REALIZE YOUR MIND IS YOUR GREATEST ASSET

Beloved, I wish above all things that you may prosper and be in health, even as your soul prospers.

—Third John : 2

It is not enough to just set goals. You must develop your mind. You mustn't waste your mind by feeding on junk. Is your mind ready for what God has in store for you? Change is the evidence of life. It is impossible to grow without change. The truth is that life is always at some turning point. As Mason has noted, "What people want is progress if they can have it without change, but that is impossible." For example, if you're going to set goals for four years, then you need to be a changed person in four years. As the literary critic Charles Augustin Sainte-Beuve has said, "There are people whose watch stops at a certain hour and who remain permanently at that age."

Don't let a day go by without reading something to develop yourself. Larry Winters has written, "You feed your body; now you've got to feed your mind." Your mind can be programmed for failure, mediocrity, or success. Life is not divided into semesters. You need to keep learning.

When was the last time you went for training specific to your trade? Derek Bok said, "If you think education is expensive, try ignorance." Some people pray to God for jobs, opportunities, and blessings that they do not have the mind to handle. Can your mind handle what you're praying to God for?

Consider Romans 12:1–3: "I beseech you therefore, brethren, by the mercies of God, that you present your bodies a living sacrifice, holy, and acceptable to God, which is your reasonable service. And do not be conformed to the world, but be transformed by the renewing of your mind, that you may prove what is that good and acceptable and perfect will of God." The Bible says that we are transformed by the renewal of our minds. The word "transformed" there comes from the same root word as the word "metamorphosis." This is similar to the transformation that the caterpillar goes through to finally become a butterfly.

Rather than trying to focus on changing ourselves, we should focus on renewing our minds, and the change will take place by itself. The Word has the power to change us, but we must be willing to allow it to change and transform us. Transformation has to start in the mind before we can change our lives. We cannot lead successful lives or careers by accident. Proverbs 23:7 says, "For as he thinks in his heart, so is he." We need to invest in the development of our minds.

KEY 24

OPPORTUNITY COMES AS ONE SKILL AWAY

Many are one skill away from great wealth.

—*Robert Kiyosaki*

Opportunity comes as developing a latent skill. According to Robert Kiyosaki, author of *Rich Dad Poor Dad*, many people are one skill away from great wealth. One skill that is crucial to develop is marketing. Another useful skill is public speaking. People are not known because they are the best writers, but because they are best sellers. You should not be too narrowly focused. You may need to learn a skill to add to your main skill that will connect you to your breakthrough. What skill do you need to learn that will put you in a different place next year? What one skill could you develop that, if added to your current skill, would move you into the top 2 percent of your professional or educational demographic?

What additional course can you take that will increase your chances of being hired or promoted? What new skill can you add to your current skills that will cause you to branch out into another field in the company and make your skill much more valuable to your organization? What added courses can you take in college that will move you to the top of the class? Anticipate, position yourself, and then take advantage of opportunity.

What one skill can change your living environment and zip code? Who do you need to partner with? What skills do you need to add to your grandma's recipe to help you open and market a restaurant?

I recently spoke with someone who was talking about a huge piece of land he owned in Lekki, a highly coveted part of Lagos, Nigeria. He said that the land was stuck in bureaucratic red tape, so he was unable to develop the land. He said his plan was to partner with someone he knew who owned a lot of properties and was familiar with the bureaucratic red tape. That way, he could get the land back, and they could share the profits. Some people will say, "It's my land, and I don't want to share the profits." Well, it was his land, and it was yielding 100 percent of the profit, which was zero. If he found a partner who could help to free up the bureaucracy and get the properties released, then he would earn a profit of, say, $1 million. Now he has 50 percent of $1 million ($500,000), just because he added one skill to his business strategy. The added skill may be something you need to develop, or it may be in someone else.

The difference between the poor and the rich is in how they think. The rich know how to harness the gifts in various people to get large projects done. The poor or mediocre rely only on their own gifts, so they do small projects, expect small, think small, speak small, and stay small. What do you need to add to your computer innovation skill that will cause Silicon Valley to start looking for you? What skill do you need to add to your love for accounting that will cause Wall Street to come knocking on your door? Opportunity comes as one skill away. You may have focused on developing and fine-tuning one skill your whole life, but it is time to see what that missing ingredient is that will bring everything together. What is that thing that moves your company from good to great? It could be a good website, a decent business card, a marketing event, a course in marketing or public speaking, or belonging to a business group or professional association. It may be speaking to mentors, business leaders, and innovators. You may be one idea away from a breakthrough. You need to believe in yourself enough to seek what is missing.

In Luke 15:11-37, the prodigal son knew there was something inside him that was yearning for a relationship that was missing. He did not let his pride get in the way. He sought that relationship out because he knew it would change his standard of living to what God had ordained for him. He knew that staying alone could not get him to where he needed and that one thing was missing. He thought he could do without that one thing but realized he needed it for restoration. He figured out a plan to get that missing thing, acted on his plan, and found his way back to his father. What relationship, idea, nugget of wisdom, or exposure is keeping you away from the expression of your gift to the world? Find it, go after it, and shine!

KEY 25

OPPORTUNITY COMES BY EXPOSING YOUR GIFT TO A DIFFERENT AUDIENCE

Give a serving to seven, and also to eight.

—Ecclesiastes 11:3

Exposing your gift to a different audience is sometimes all you need for a breakthrough. As Ecclesiastes 11:6 teaches us: "In the morning sow your seed, and in the evening do not withhold your hand; for you do not know which will prosper, either this or that." The Bible says to give a serving to seven, and also to eight (meaning we should sow seed in different places). We are sometimes one audience short of a breakthrough. It is not that you need another product, talent, or gift; you just need one more audience to show it to. You need one more investor to pitch your idea to. You need one more avenue to expose your gift to. Your gift may be worth a high amount in one setting and a low amount in another.

As a psychiatrist, depending on where I work, the rate is different. I keep taking advantage of different opportunities to use my gift and to expose it to different audiences. For me to fully utilize my gift, I have to be willing to work in different settings in order to maximize the exposure. The Bible says that you do not know what evil shall come upon the earth, or which one shall prosper, either this or that. I like to say it this way: sometimes you need to go after "this and that."

The Bible encourages us to be open to sowing our seed in different settings. This doesn't necessarily mean that we need to have seven or eight jobs, but it means we need to be open to exposing our gifts to different audiences and to not be stuck in a rut.

God acknowledges that evil will come on the earth—your favorite boss could leave, management could change, the company could close down or be bought out, or the need for a product may dry up five years from now in your location. You need to be able to discern changes in the market and be sensitive to the leading of God's spirit. If God is speaking to your heart to expand your horizon, then you need to do so.

You don't determine the location of your blessing; you determine the extent of your obedience.

Are you willing to expose your gift to a different audience? In 1 Kings 17:5–15, Elijah had to move from the brook and expose his gift to the widow for continued provision. God wanted to bless Elijah, and the season of him being fed by the brook was over. What if he had started a congregation by the brook and told God that he did not want to abandon his congregation? Well, he would have missed out on God's provision because the brook would have dried up. Sometimes the brook dries up because God has ended that season and wants to bring you into another season. If you've built a monument where God asked you to build a tent, then you will become a pillar of salt because you'll keep looking back when God tells you to move on—just like in the story of Lot's wife in Sodom and Gomorrah (Luke 17:32).

Are you obedient to what God is saying? We need to be sensitive to the spirit of God and allow Him to direct us to maximize our gifting. Ecclesiastes 11:4–6 says, "He who observes the wind will not sow, and he who regards the clouds will not reap." There are always obstacles to sowing as well as to reaping, for you do not know which shall prosper or whether both shall be good. In your spare time, you may start something because you want to be a blessing to others, but that could blossom into a wonderful opportunity. The client you least expect may be the one who gives you the largest return. Prosperity comes when you expose your talent to a different audience. Be broad-minded in your target audience. In the age of the internet and Facebook, you have the potential to reach a wide audience. Be open to a new set of clientele, and do not be too restrictive in your vision. Don't limit your audience, because one way in which God increases you is by increasing your territory. You increase your territory by increasing your audience. Some people don't want to enlarge their territory, but they expect God to work within the limited confines they have set for Him. But opportunity comes when we expose our gift to a different audience. God wants us to expand our vision. In Genesis 13:15, God told Abraham, "Look...for all the land which you see I give to you and your descendants forever." Your perception is your limitation. You have to see possibilities and opportunities, in order to experience them.

KEY 26

OPPORTUNITY COMES AS A TRADE SECRET

He made known His ways unto Moses,
His acts unto the children of Israel.

—*Psalm 103:7*

God can give you a secret to a particular market. This could be an unusual understanding in your field of endeavor. We need to stay open to divine revelations, which don't have to be spectacular to be supernatural. He can give you a secret approach to your business, parenting, debt elimination, or healing a broken relationship.

Never start any day with a sense of dread. God can give you a revelation that can thrust you years ahead in one moment. It is important to stay open. There are things that come very easy to you but that are very valuable to others. That is part of your secret. Coca-Cola has a secret ingredient. What is yours? Can God trust you with a secret? Proverbs 3:20 says, "By His knowledge the depths are broken up, and the clouds drop down the dew." You need to realize that you have access to the secret truths of the kingdom. Such secrets could simply be ways to improve on things that already exist, or they could be knowing where to buy something cheap and to sell it for a profit. The secret could be a recipe. It could be knowing the marketing formula for a business. It could be creating apps. You may find it while in search of something else, but because you remain open-minded, you accidentally discover it. We tend to undervalue ourselves and overvalue what others possess. God can reveal a secret to you that can change your life.

In Genesis 30, Jacob was given a secret formula that helped him to get out from under the reign of Laban (The father of his future wife, Rachel). He had fourteen years till he finally got Rachel, his wife. After that, he asked when he could leave and go start his family but Laban was not willing to let him go easily. He then proposed a formula that led to significant increase because God told him a secret about how to get the cattle to mate in order to obtain the results that were favorable to him. God can stack the decks in your favor. If He gave success to Jacob, then He can give it to you. God can give you a secret ingredient that will take you from employee to owner. We have to be willing to ask for that secret ingredient and to step out in it.

KEY 27

OPPORTUNITY COMES BY PUTTING THE KINGDOM FIRST

But seek first the kingdom of God, and His righteousness;
and all these things shall be added unto you.

—Matthew 6:33

What priority does God have in your life? Are you running after things, or are you running after God? Mathew 6:33 states, "But seek first the kingdom of God and His righteousness, and all these things will be added to you." Sometimes what we need is not more things but a change in our priorities—putting God first and seeing ourselves as vessels for a greater purpose. The Bible says that we should seek the kingdom and its righteousness first, and all these things will then be added to us.

True success comes when we seek God first. God's plan is for things to be added to you, not that you will just chase things. Does this mean we should not strive to improve our lives? Does this mean we should not desire to prosper? No, Third John Verse 2 says "Beloved, I pray that you may prosper and be in health, just as your soul prospers" God wants prosperity to be our portion but not at the expense of our spiritual growth.

Mark 8:36 asks, "For what will it profit a man if he gains the whole world, and loses his own soul or what will a man give in exchange for his soul?" There is no profit in focusing on gaining wealth at the expense of your spiritual growth. Money can buy a lot of things, but some things cannot be bought. Putting the kingdom of God first means placing a priority on our relationship with God. It means keeping things in perspective. We see the story of Mary and Martha in Luke 10:38–43. Martha was worried and preoccupied with many legitimate things, such as taking care of what Jesus was going to eat. "But Martha was distracted by much serving and she approached Him and said, 'Lord, do you not care that my sister has left me to serve alone? Tell her to help me.' And Jesus answered and said to her, 'Martha, Martha, you are worried and troubled about many things. But one thing is needed, and Mary has chosen that good part, which will not be taken from her." Martha was focused on the cares of the world, but Jesus said that Mary had chosen the good part.

The kingdom is always going to be on a list of choices. God is not going to choose for you. The kingdom remains the good part, but you have to choose the kingdom. When we put that choice first, we see that we live a life of peace and contentment, we walk in forgiveness, we have a genuine love for people, we are patient in trying circumstances, and we treat people the way we want to be treated. We also do not try to live our lives according to the Joneses. Seeking the kingdom first helps us to see that we have a responsibility beyond this world and the people around us—we are accountable to God through our conscience. Knowing that we are going to give an account of our actions helps to put things in perspective. Seeking the kingdom first means living a principled life based on the Word of God. It means allowing the Word of God, not culture, to shape your beliefs. As a Christian, I aim to allow the Word of God to be my standard in situations in my life.

Being planted in a local church is extremely important. Consider Psalm 92:13: "Those who are planted in the house of the Lord shall flourish in the courts of our God. They shall still bear fruit in old age; they shall be fresh and flourishing." You may be wondering what all this has to do with opportunity, but not all opportunity is God-given opportunity. The enemy gives you a lot of opportunities to derail your life and to knock God out of first place. That is why we need to make sure that our hearts are in the right place so that we can truly discern which opportunities God has given us. The fact that something is a good idea does not mean that it is a God-given idea. Being grounded spiritually allows you to determine what good opportunities are and what are not. Romans 14:17 says, "For the kingdom of God is not eating and drinking, but righteousness and peace and joy in the Holy Spirit." Place priority on God's kingdom. True life comes when we have a relationship with our creator and live out His purpose for our lives.

KEY 28

OPPORTUNITY COMES WHEN YOU COME TO YOURSELF AND THINK DIFFERENTLY

But when he came to himself he...

—*Luke 15:17*

Look at the prodigal son: when he came to himself, he thought differently. There are times when you need to assess where you are in life. You will need to think differently. Proverbs 23:7 says, "For as he thinks in his heart, so is he." If you're going to excel in life, then you have to be prepared to change the way you think.

You cannot think defeat and expect success. You cannot think failure and expect victory. You cannot meditate on anxiety and expect peace. Ward stated that "nothing limits achievement like small thinking: nothing expands possibilities like unleashed imagination." As Philippians 4:8 says, "Finally, brethren, whatsoever things are true, whatsoever things are honest, whatsoever things are just, whatsoever things are pure, whatsoever things are lovely, whatsoever things are of good report; if there be any virtue, if there be any praise, think on these things." What are you thinking about? You do have control over what you choose to meditate on. As

Proverbs 4:23 teaches us, "Keep your heart with all diligence, for out of it springs the issues of life."

This means that what you meditate on will shape your life and experience. Your life for the most part will not be a surprise to you. That is why the Bible says to keep your heart with all diligence. You should put effort into guarding what you meditate and think on. You need to think on purpose, not by accident and not based on how you feel. That means you can feel one way and yet program your mind to think another way; then the feelings will follow.

Don't let your feelings take the lead; you take the lead by thinking and speaking the right things. The way you guard your heart is by guarding what you look at, what you think of, and then what you say. The key from Philippians 4:8 is not just avoiding the wrong things but thinking on the right things. Think about what you are thinking about.

As Luke 6:45 says, "A good man out of the good treasure of his heart brings forth good; and an evil man out of the evil treasure of his heart brings forth evil. For out of the abundance of the heart his mouth speaks." What you have in your heart in abundance will eventually come out of your lips.

Joshua 1:8 says, "This Book of the Law shall not depart from your mouth, but you shall meditate in it day and night, that you may observe to do according to all that is written in it. For then you will make your way prosperous, and then you will have good success." We need to be diligent in putting the Word into our hearts, which influences what we meditate on. We live in a very negative world, and we won't think about positive things by accident. You must purposefully meditate on the Word of God in order to see the fruit borne in your life.

KEY 29

OPPORTUNITY COMES THROUGH SERVICE

He who is faithful in what is least is faithful also in much;
and he who is unjust in what is least is unjust also in much.

—Luke 16:10

Some people consider certain roles too small for them. They feel they are
not in the spotlight. They don't see serving people as enough of a blessing. But it is important that you see greatness in everything you do. No
matter how small what you are doing seems or who is watching you, you
need to be faithful in it. Look at the parable of the talents in Matthew
25:14–30. Their master gave them money according to their abilities, and
he expected them to trade with it and be faithful in what he gave them.
When he came back, the one he'd given five talents had traded with it and
made five more talents. The one he'd given two talents had traded with it
and gained two more talents. The one he'd given one talent hid it and gave
it back to his lord. Their lord commended the two who'd traded with their
talents: "Well done, good and faithful servant; you were faithful over a few
things, I will make you ruler over many things. Enter into the joy of your
lord." To the one who'd given him back the talent, he said, "You wicked
and lazy servant, you knew that I reap where I have not sown, and gather

where I have not scattered seed. So you ought to have deposited my money with the bankers, and at my coming I would have received back my own with interest. Therefore take the talent from him, and give it to him who has ten talents. For to everyone who has, more will be given, and he will have abundance; but from him who does not have, even what he has will be taken away."

God wants us to be faithful in the little things. If you cannot serve people, then you cannot serve God. Whatever God has given you, do it to the best of your ability. Ecclesiastes 9:10 says, "Whatever your hand finds to do, do it with your might." Do things with excellence. Do things as unto the Lord and not as to other people. It is important to see service as a key factor in developing opportunity. If you have looked for work and could not find it, then volunteer. Many people have discovered job opportunities through volunteering. As Acts 20:35 says, "It is more blessed to give than to receive." Do something to improve someone else's life. Some people are waiting for the perfect job, not knowing that opportunity can come through volunteering.

Opportunity can also come through doing your best in whatever situation or job you find yourself in. You don't know which customer will write a review about you that will lead to a promotion or recognition. Many people remain stagnant even in church because they haven't found their ideal place to serve. You need to start somewhere, and then God will illuminate your path. If you are faithful in little things, then you will be faithful in much bigger things (Luke 19:17). Many people do not want to start little. Similarly, many are unemployed because they don't have the perfect job. It is important that you are in the workforce, even if you're volunteering. You will miss certain relationships, contacts, and encounters if you are not in the workforce. Volunteering even looks good on your résumé, since doing so shows that you are industrious.

When administration is looking for someone to put in a paid position, who do you think they will look to first? It will be the person whose work ethic they already know, and is a team player. They figure that, if you can do something with diligence when you're not getting paid, then you'll do it with at least the same (if not more) diligence when you are getting paid.

The same thing is true in the church setting: you begin to volunteer wherever there is a need, such as working as a greeter, and they then begin to see your dedication, commitment, leadership, and servant heart, and before you know it, they begin to give you more responsibilities until you're in a place where you're using more of your gift. In the meantime, you're being a blessing.

Any work you do in the house of God is a blessing to the kingdom, and all roles are of equal importance. You should serve, not just because you want to be in the spotlight but because opportunity comes through service and because you are being obedient to God.

KEY 30

OPPORTUNITY COMES BY SEIZING THE RIGHT MOMENT

*Arise, shine; For your light has come! And the
glory of the Lord is risen upon you.*

—Isaiah 60:1

It is important that we maintain a heart of expectation. There are times when God will tell us to do things when the circumstances are not ideal. If we are too consumed with the circumstances we are in, we will not seize the moment. Mark 5:25–34 tells of a woman with a flow of blood for twelve years. She seized her moment. She'd had a blood-related problem for twelve years, but she did not let that be the defining problem in her life. When she heard of Jesus, she said to herself, "If I may but touch the hem of His garment, I will be made whole."

She had been ill for many years and had had her expectations crushed over and over again after going to many physicians but yet became worse. The Bible says that when she heard of Jesus, she knew there was a period in time when He was going to be passing by. She saw the people all around Jesus, but she did not let that stop her. Some people were there to see Jesus, and some people wanted to be in the crowd, but she knew what she wanted: she wanted her healing. She said all she needed to do was to touch the hem of His garment. The Bible says she pressed through the crowd with persistence and determination. She did not wait for Jesus to call her; she was not in His direct path, and she did not wait for someone to carry her to Jesus. She pressed through the crowd and touched the hem of His garment.

She did not allow the years of disappointment to make her miss her moment. She did not allow her doubts to keep her stuck in a rut. She nurtured her hope and changed what she was saying, and when the specified time for her healing came, she exercised her faith in the mode of healing of her choosing. She touched the hem of His garment. That's why the Bible records that Jesus said, "Your faith has made you whole." Jesus had the power, but it was her faith that caused the power to flow out of Jesus and into her body.

Sometimes we are so busy in preparation that we don't know when our moment is here. Isaiah 60:1 says, "Arise, shine; for your light has come!" Has your light come? When revelation dawns on your heart about a particular problem, be obedient to what instructions come into your heart. Isaiah 1:19 says, "If you are willing and obedient, you shall eat the good of the land." Many people are willing, but few are able to seize their moments of opportunity. You don't have to ask yourself, "What are the circumstances saying?" Sometimes your moment comes because God reveals it to you. Sometimes your moment comes because you receive a revelation or understanding about a particular problem, and acting on that knowledge opens doors for you. At other times, a favorable moment opens to us at a time we did not expect, but that is why it is important to have our expectations on all the time. Unless God has given you a particular time frame, you should not place yourself in one. You should always have an expectation that a miracle can happen today.

KEY 31

OPPORTUNITY COMES THROUGH PERSISTENCE

Through faith and patience they inherit the promises.

—*Hebrews 6:12*

Hebrews 10:35 states, "Therefore do not cast away your confidence, which has great reward. For you have need of endurance, so that after you have done the will of God, you may receive the promise." It is not enough to have faith; we need to have patience to inherit the promise. Circumstances come to try our faith. Consider James 1:2-3: "Count it all joy when you fall into various trials, knowing that the testing of your faith produces patience." Situations and trials come to test your faith to see if you will give up on the promise. We need to hold on to the promise despite the opposition. That was what Isaac did in the face of opposition.

Genesis 26:17–22 says,

> "Then Isaac departed from there and pitched his tent in the Valley of Gerar, and dwelt there. And Isaac dug again the wells of water which they had dug in the days of Abraham his father...But the herdsmen of Gerar quarreled

with Isaac's herdsmen, saying, "The water is ours." So he called the name of the well Esek, because they quarreled with him. Then they dug another well, and they quarreled over that one also. So he called its name Sitnah. And he moved from there and dug another well, and they did not quarrel over it. So he called its name Rehoboth, because he said, "For now the Lord has made room for us, and we shall be fruitful in the land."

Isaac was persistent in digging wells. He did not give up because the first two did not work out. He knew he had a promise, and he kept doing his part, taking actions that corresponded with his faith. God could be saying to you, "Dig another well." He kept walking by faith and not allowing the opposition to stop him from taking steps toward his promise. He eventually saw his promise realized. He did not become bitter at people; because he knew the promise was greater than the opposition.

We also see Abraham in Romans 4:13–21:

(As it is written, "I have made you a father of many nations") in the presence of Him whom he believed—God, who gives life to the dead and calls those things which do not exist as though they did; who, contrary to hope, in hope believed, so that he became the father of many nations, according to what was spoken, "So shall your descendants be." And not being weak in faith, he did not consider his own body, already dead (since he was about a hundred years old), and the deadness of Sarah's womb. He did not waver at the promise of God through unbelief, but was strengthened in faith, giving glory to God, and being fully convinced that what He had promised He was also able to perform."

The Bible says that Abraham did not waver at the promise of God that he would be the father of many nations. He was strengthened in faith, giving glory to God, and was fully convinced. Abraham was an excellent example of opportunity coming through patience. He was given an impossible promise at an impossible time of his life. When he was younger, his wife was barren. The Lord then appeared to him in his later years, stating that he would father a son. He waited for twenty-five years to realize the promise. It was ridiculous when he first heard the promise and more ridiculous when the promise was actually fulfilled.

But how often do we give up after a week, a month, a year, or a few years? We stand in faith for a while and then give up. We see that Abraham was not just "white-knuckling" it for twenty-five years. We see that he was strengthened in faith and giving glory to God. We see that his trust in God was not static through the years; his faith continued to grow. His faith grew to where he was fully convinced. He got to the point where his faith was no longer dependent on time but on God. As long as he was alive, he was in faith. He did not allow time to steal an iota of his faith. As a matter of fact, the more time passed, the more convinced he was, and he was strengthened in giving glory to God. How glorious it would be if we could all walk in patience after receiving the promise.

It is possible. Through faith and patience, we inherit the promise!

ABOUT THE AUTHOR

Lanre Somorin MD is a board-certified psychiatrist and has been practicing since 1995. He is also an associate pastor. He has a specialty in Addiction Psychiatry. Somorin's mission is to help people discover hope and to live purposeful lives.

He has been listed in the Top Doctors' issue of the Hudson Valley Magazine yearly since 2006. He owned and operated an outpatient substance abuse rehab facility and has held various leadership positions, including clinical consultant to the Army Substance Abuse Clinic in West Point, NY. He is currently practicing in Orange County, NY. He has been married for twenty-three years and is the father of two.

For more information please visit seizeyoumomentnow.com

REFERENCES

Dictionary.com. s.v. "Opportunity." Accessed October 10, 2017. http://www.dictionary.com/browse/opportunity?s=t.

Kiyosaki, Robert T. 2011. *Rich Dad Poor Dad: What the Rich Teach Their Kids about Money That the Poor and Middle Class Do Not!* Scottsdale, AZ: Plata.

Mason, John. 1996. *Conquering an Enemy Called Average*. Tulsa, OK: Insight International.

Oyedepo, David O. 1996. *The Force of Freedom*. Lagos, Nigeria: Dominion Publishing.

Winters, Larry. 2012. *Live the Dream: No More Excuses*. New York: Center Street.

Prayer to Welcome Jesus Christ as Your Lord and Savior (Rom. 10:9–10)

Father, thank you for sending your son, Jesus, to die for me on the cross. I believe in my heart that Jesus is the son of God, that He died on the cross, and that He rose again from the dead. I confess that He is my Lord and Savior. I commit my life to you; come into my life and be my Lord and Savior.

In Jesus' name, amen.

28176037R00052